# APPLEDORE, NORTHAM & WESTWARD HO! THROUGH THE LENS

Peter Christie
&
Pat Slade

Edward Gaskell *publishers*
DEVON

First published 2011
Edward Gaskell *publishers*
The Old Gazette Building
6 Grenville Street
Bideford
Devon
EX39 2EA


isbn (10) 1-906769-28-1
isbn (13) 978-1-906769-28-4

APPLEDORE, NORTHAM & WESTWARD HO!
THROUGH THE LENS

Peter Christie
& Pat Slade

Typeset, printed and bound by
Lazarus Press
Caddsdown Business Park
Bideford
Devon
EX39 3DX
www.lazaruspress.com

# Contents

APPLEDORE                                    7

NORTHAM                                     75

WESTWARD HO!                           119

*Lazarus Press*
DEVON

# Introduction

It is perhaps odd that none of the three places dealt with in this book has attracted a full history as of yet - Appledore is a fascinating maritime village, Northam is an ancient settlement, whilst Westward Ho! is a very unusual Victorian 'new town'. We feel certain that one day they will get the treatment they deserve - and one aspect of this will be illustrations and this is where this book comes in. Both authors have previously published photographic histories of Bideford so a companion volume to that town's neighbours seemed an obvious next step. Drawing on our personal collections of photographs and those lent by others we have compiled this volume. Whilst putting it together we have realised that we will probably have enough for a second volume, so if this one proves popular there may well be a follow up. We would of course welcome any contributions from others so if you do have any photographs you think would be of interest then please contact either of us:

Peter Christie - 9 Kenwith Road, Bideford EX39 3NW, 01237 473577
Pat Slade - 86 Atlantic Way Westward Ho! EX39 1JG 01237 474946

Photographs have been lent to the authors by the following people who retain the copyright:

| | |
|---|---|
| R. Boucher | T. Hatton |
| G. Braddick | T. Jarvis |
| H. Cleaver | J. Mackie |
| P. Cloke | North Devon Athenaeum |
| C. Cock | North Devon Journal |
| D. Cole | J. Plumtree |
| E. Gordon | C. Wood |

**The Front Cover:** shows the Bleriot monoplane flown around England in June 1912 by French pilot M.Salmet after he had landed on Northam Burrows near the Pebble Ridge Hotel. He was met by a huge crowd who had travelled to see him via the Bideford, Westward Ho! and Appledore Railway, cars and carriages. Local police and Boy Scouts kept the area clear and he was greeted by W.T.Goaman, Mayor of Bideford. After staying a few days he flew on to Bude.

Edward Gaskell *publishers*

# Appledore

*Above*: Appledore Quay sometime around 1900. The cart to the right was used to carry luggage from holidaymakers who had arrived by train at Instow and crossed the river using the rowing boat ferry.

*Next page*: Aerial views are always full of interest and this 1920s one of Appledore shows a host of sailing vessels moored up off the Quay and Richmond Dock. The long gardens on the left which provided much garden produce to their owners stand out clearly.

APPLEDORE from the Air.

OLD STREET IN APPLEDORE.

Irsha Street is famous for its small cottages and here we see some of them before they were modernised and turned into second or holiday homes. The cobblestones in the street have long been tarmaced over.

*Meeting Street, Appledore*

*Above*: Another of Appledore's small cobbled streets. Meeting Street was so called because it housed an old religious meeting house which later became the Congregational chapel.

*Next page*: Clearly the presence of a photographer caused the crowd of children (and a few adults) to materialise and fill the shot. The sign board of the still existing 'Champion of Wales' is very prominent - and note the thin layer of tarmac over the road cobbles.

This amateur photograph was taken from an upstairs window in Bude Street probably sometime just after the First World War. The house on the right was the old village police station - with two cells at the rear.

Hillcliff Terrace, Appledore is still recognisable today but the railings seen in this photograph were removed as part of the Second World War 'War Effort'. During the war two 4.7 inch naval guns were sited on the green area in front of the terrace to guard the estuary entrance. The central door of the three used to house the Trinity House buoys put out to mark the navigation channel.

This small corner shop run by the Land family was typical of the many local village shops in Appledore. As with so many the building has now become an art and craft shop. The postcard was sent in January 1906.

Evidently everyone wanted to be in this photograph. It was taken around 1902 in Market Street, Appledore. The curious 'globe' on the skyline was atop the old Rechabite Hall.

The narrowness of Marine Parade in Appledore with bollards to make it even narrower will surprise modern users today. The vessels on the left are sitting in Richmond Dock whilst the building in the centre (at the bottom of Silver Street) was demolished to widen the road.

This is thought to show One End Street in Appledore with one of the many small 'front room' shops that used to be so common in our towns and villages. Note the cobbled street - the photograph probably dates from around 1900.

Land's Series

Odun Road, Appledore with the grand Odun House (with porch) in the centre. This was once the house of the Reverend Jerome Clapp (father of Jerome K.Jerome) and later became the Appledore Maritime Museum. The railings all went for wartime salvage but the Museum has replaced theirs with ones from the defunct Westward Ho! pier.

*Above*: This rare view of Pitt in Appledore dates from the very early 1900s. The absence of any building on the left of the road makes the view unusual to us today.

*Next page*: As with many old settlements Appledore had a small market. This was located at the end of Market Street where it extended to the Quay. As can be seen it was only partially covered with a bench for the stallholders opposite some small lock-up shops.

Market Place Appledore.

WESTWARD HO FROM APPLEDORE

3714

A close-up view of the Appledore Lifeboat slipway which is locally known as Badstep. The interest in the photograph comes not just from this but also from the three tall wartime radar masts on Northam Burrows in the background.

Looking down Market Street in the 1950s. The Globe Hotel provided valuable accommodation to early tourists to the village.

A view of Irsha Street this time towards the north-western end sometime in the 1950s. At one time two-way traffic ran down the road - including small buses!

Another view of Irsha Street looking in the same direction to the previous one. This dates from the 1950s and shows the long gone Rising Sun Inn which was opposite the old Gaiety Cinema which has also disappeared.

Chanter's Folly in Appledore was a famous landmark built by local merchant Thomas Chanter in 1819 and provided a look out for him to spot his homecoming vessels. The mother of Pat Slade, one of the authors of this book, used to regularly visit the Folly to see whether the m.v. *Lerina*, the Lundy supply vessel, was coming over the Bar in order to have her husband's dinner ready by the time the vessel docked and he came ashore. The Folly was hit by lightning in 1927, damaged by fire in 1945 and demolished in 1952.

This fine aerial view of part of Appledore Quay dates from the early 1950s when the area next to the church was still all allotments. The presence of just two cars and one bus is surprising to us today, used as we are, to crowded roads and a mass of parked cars. Note the imposing bulk of the old Independent Chapel in the top left - where the Reverend Jerome Clapp, father of Jerome K.Jerome, was once minister.

The beginning of Irsha Street in Appledore once housed the boatbuilding yard of H. Ford whose nameboard is seen in this shot from the early 1950s. The small building to the left was the old toilet block and now is used by the local sub-aqua diving club to store equipment.

The Promenade in Appledore showing the old swimming pool sometime in the early 1950s. Owing to an outbreak of polio in the village, the pool, which was thought to be a source of the infection, was removed.

This panoramic view of Appledore from Instow was taken in the 1970s and shows the Quay before its most recent widening. The old village frontage contrasts strongly with the later housing developments on the hill behind - with the houses interspersed with gardens and seemingly random open spaces.

*Above*: Appledore is an old fishing community with hardly a straight or wide road in it - and consequently the growth of modern road traffic has seen major problems develop over parking. In February 1990 the authorities began work on a large new car park. Costing some £656,000 it was due to be completed in August of that year and here we see it at the half way mark. Unfortunately Appledore residents have tended to prefer parking on the road (free) to parking in the car park (paid for) and one wonders if the building costs have been covered even today?

*Next page*: This unusual view of Appledore was taken by a group of intrepid climbers from Skern Lodge in September 1990. They had climbed a huge crane at Appledore Shipyard and then abseiled down to raise funds for the village Youth Club's plan to build a children's park on the Quay in the then new car park.

6156. The Quay, Appledore.

Appledore Quay before it was widened in 1938. Previous attempts to carry out the widening foundered on a lack of agreement between the householders along the Quay all of whom had rights over the area.

Appledore had a very long and proud tradition of links to the sea and it was rare for any photograph not to include one or two vessels at least. Note the rather uneven road surface and puddles.

This unusual view of some very typical coasting vessels at Appledore was clearly taken by an adventurous photographer from a boat. The shot predates the 1938 widening of the Quay.

The Appledore-Instow ferry has had a long and intriguing history. Here we see one of the ferry boats in the early 1930s. The inscription on the boat reads 'Mona. W. Bailey. Appledore' whilst the one next to it is called 'Enterprise'. The old rowing boat ferry now seems to have disappeared for ever and recent attempts to replace it with an amphibious DUKW ferry have run into problems.

The shore at Appledore before the Quay was widened is caught well in this photograph from the early 1930s. The beach has gone today having been covered by the new promenade and though the small boats are still there the graceful wooden sailing vessels have long disappeared from our coastal waters.

The Quay, Appledore.

Sails have given way to steel and engines in this shot from the late 1940s. The two landing craft were probably based at the Amphibious Warfare establishment at Instow just opposite.

*Above*: Today's lifeboat house at Appledore is a massive structure of steel and granite unlike its predecessor shown here in the 1930s which was built of local stone and wood. Standing in front of the large doors is Tom Hornabrook the engineer for the lifeboat inside - and father of Pat Slade co-author of this book.

*Next page*: Tom is shown with the boarding boat used to row out to the lifeboat floating behind him - this being the *Violet Armstrong*.

The *Stan Woolaway* in the centre of this shot was launched as a gravel dredger for a firm of Barnstaple based builders but sank in March 1967 off Morthoe. The two sailing vessels moored alongside Appledore Quay are the *Irene* and *Emily Barrett*.

This photograph was a proof copy produced prior to mass production and clearly shows the widened Appledore Quay - and note the presence of the Hocking's ice cream van in the centre - with the *Kathleen & May* moored alongside.

For most of its history Appledore has been a shipbuilding port - with shipborne trade being fairly small. In April 1954 the m.v. *Irene* was photographed discharging animal feed at the village Quay - it being only the second vessel to discharge at Appledore Quay since 1945!

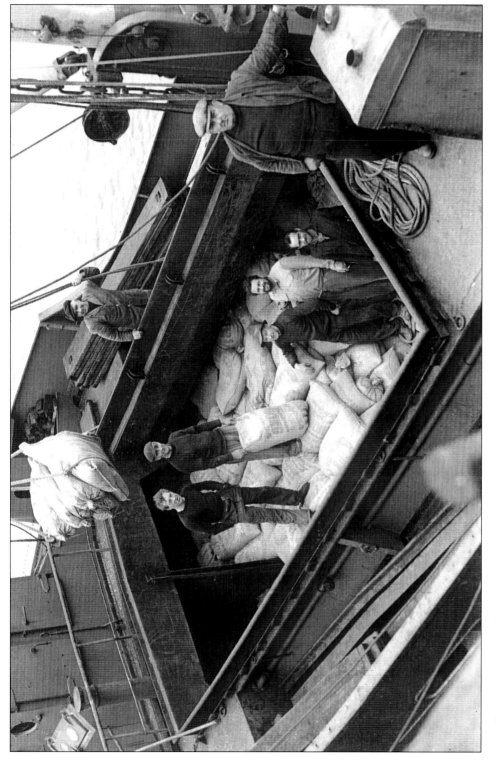

Another cargo arrived in February 1955 consisting rather oddly of oyster shells brought in to feed local poultry.

The instantly recognisable schooner the *Kathleen & May* snapped alongside Appledore Quay in June 1967. She was sailed into the port by Captain Paul Davis after he found her lying derelict in Southampton Water and purchased her - raising the price by selling his insurance policies, premium bonds and 2 cars. Of course, since then, she has been refitted, become a derelict once

In 1962 Appledore Shipyard workers built the *Kpeshie* fishing boat for newly-independent Ghana at a cost of £180,000. Unfortunately the Ghanaian government had a change of policy and decided they didn't want the boat. It was thus tied up in Appledore and left in limbo for 2 years until April 1964 when she was taken in tow by a tug up to Hull where she was to be sold. Luckily a photographer was on hand to record the ignominious departure.

*Above*: Although this hovercraft wasn't built in Appledore it was brought to the port in February 1968 to be evaluated by the Instow amphibious warfare testing unit in heavy surf conditions in the estuary. Unfortunately the sea was totally calm all during the time set aside for the testing!

*Next page*: This old barge was photographed in July 1987 at the Hubbastone patent slip in Appledore. It was the *Advance* which had been built at Appledore by P.K. Harris & Sons in 1926 for the Devon Trading Company to supply their Barnstaple and Bideford outlets with sand and gravel from the local estuary. She had been rescued by Captain Peter Herbert and he was engaged in restoring her.

*Above*: This is an extraordinary photograph. Taken in August 1969 at Appledore Shipyard it shows the Shellmex/BP Ltd tanker *Poilo* being altered from an 800 tonner to one of 1000 tons. This was achieved by the simple expedient of cutting the vessel in half and inserting a new 20 foot central section. Lengthening took just 3 weeks and the shipyard had orders for four other operations. Once finished the vessels were returned to the Thames estuary where they helped refuel large seagoing tankers.

*Next page*: Appledore Shipyard under a variety of owners has been the life blood of the village for many decades now and to cement the links the yard occasionally holds an 'Open Day'. This photograph shows one such from April 1987 when a new £7 million dredger the *Arco-Arun* was being completed. The gentleman in the picture is Roy Henstridge the safety and security officer of the yard.

*Above*: This photograph shows the launch of the *Manchester Vigour* from Appledore Shipyard in March 1973. Noted as 'the largest vessel yet to be built on the Torridge' it had only 3" clearance as it left the dock - and it certainly looks that room was extremely tight!

*Next page*: We see a real contrast between the old and the new. It is May 1973. The old was the replica of the Elizabethan vessel *The Golden Hinde* which was built at Appledore, and the new was the giant crane in Appledore Shipyard which was being used to lower the foremast into the vessel. Over the next few days both the mizzen and bowsprit were also put into place. The second photo shows the vessel with the masts in position. Costing some £250,000 the ship had been built for some San Francisco owners who planned to sail her across the Atlantic for use as a tourist attraction.

In 1974 work was going on to build the Thorpe Water Park leisure centre in Surrey. As part of the planned attractions a Viking ship was to be installed - and the order for its construction went to Appledore shipbuilders J.Hinks & Son. Famous for several other reproduction old vessels the Viking example is seen here under construction at their yard in December 1974.

A photograph showing Appledore shipyard in its heyday. It shows the *Britannia Beaver* built at a cost of £9 million in 1990. Owned by Britannia Aggregates Ltd. it was launched by Emma Nicholson the Torridge MP famous, or infamous, as Torridge's turncoat MP. At the time of this shot the shipyard was also working on a 4500 tonne bulk carrier with 3 liquid gas carriers on order thus giving a combined order book of some £44.5 million.

This marvellous looking car, decorated for a wedding, was picture in Marine Parade, Appledore around 1910. Robert Lamey is the driver seated outside what was then a confectionery shop and what today is an antique shop.

These three men in their bus driver's caps were employed on the Bideford-Appledore routes in the 1920s. The photograph below shows them again this time with their vehicles - which prompts one to ask where did all these splendid old buses go?

*Above*: This picture has one of the local buses making its way somewhat gingerly from Marine Parade to Myrtle Street in Appledore. The strange outdoor 'curtain' over the window was a sun shade protecting the sweet shop behind which has now been demolished.

*Next page*: The shortage of houses after the Second World War was acute for many years and in North Devon Appledore Shipbuilders, looking to expand their business, had decided to experiment with prefabricated houses. This shot shows the first one erected inside the shipyard prior to being put up (in just 4 days) in the village in March 1964. Local builders who had viewed the new house were 'impressed by the quality of workmanship'.

*Above*: Your eyes aren't deceiving you - this is a car driving in the water. Taken at Appledore in January 1968 it reflects the resourcefulness of Jim Venus managing director of Appledore Shipbuilders who, when part of Bideford Bridge collapsed in 1968, decided to buy an amphibious car to allow him to cross the Torridge without being inconvenienced by the 25 mile detour then in place.

*Next page*: An Appledore Carnival parade probably in the early 1950s. In the top photograph a large number of walking characters are seen at the entrance to the park - the present-day Churchfields car park is to the left. On the lower photograph the maritime theme is very evident - with masses of what looks like seaweed decorating the float.

A 1953 street party in Appledore to mark the coronation of Queen Elizabeth II in that year. Note the sleeveless jumpers on the boys and the masses of ship's flags used as bunting.

Appledore Regatta in July 1954 when Miss Sylvia Passmore of Barnstaple was selected as 'Queen' with 4 attendants - Hester Sanders, Elizabeth Branch, June Pike & Sheila Pascoe. The specially decorated boat was manned by Harold Stevens and Ian Cox.

*Above*: A rather prosaic backdrop for an exotic carnival float in this photograph from Appledore in 1957. A group of ladies under Kathleen Jarvis had got together to recreate the characters from Puccini's 'Madam Butterfly'. Along with Kathleen there was Sylvia Down, Valerie Hocking, Mary Jarvis, Valerie and Mary Eastman, Pat Tilte and Sylvia Squire - some good old Appledore names there! They do not seem to have been among the prize winners having been beaten by one intriguing float from the village's Darby and Joan Club which featured seven women whose combined age came to 521!

*Next page*: We are not sure who the lucky man is in this photograph from August 1964 but he is looking quite happy to be carrying the Appledore Regatta Queen Veronica Squires ashore at Instow from what appears to be the Appledore-Instow ferry boat. The regatta itself was well attended with the Bideford Blues beating Dartmouth in the final of the rowing races.

This float from the 1964 Appledore Carnival was titled 'Wales for ever'. It was put together by four Appledore families, under the leadership of Mrs. E. Edwards, and won the prize for the 'Best decorated lorry - Open Tableaux'. Note the impressive 'Welsh Dresser' at the back of the lorry.

*Above*: In June 1968 Appledore Shipbuilders Ltd. presented a cheque for £1000 to Appledore's playing field appeal. This, along with the money already collected, was enough to lay out a play area at Anchor Park. This included a sand pit, pitches for netball and football and an adventure playground. Cyril Cox of Bideford presented a 2 ton anchor from the nineteenth century barque *Falkirk* to the committee managing the fund and this photograph records its positioning by 18 employees of the shipyard.

*Next page*: North Devon's coastline is no stranger to gales and heavy seas but only rarely does the sea wreak such damage as it did in February 1967. The usually well protected village of Appledore was hit by huge waves so much so that part of the stone sea wall near the old Gaiety Cinema collapsed - as shown in this photograph taken from the beach. We think the gentleman in the black raincoat is Bill Ford though we could be wrong. The second picture was taken a few weeks later and shows rebuilding work beginning.

This intriguing photograph was taken in Appledore in December 1974 and records the village's 'Pirates' charity fund raising group parading with some 150 blazing torches through the streets just prior to a carol service around a Christmas tree they had erected in Appledore Park. Sadly the tree was minus its lights they having been stolen but this didn't dampen the occasion which was notable for the men stopping outside Bradbourne House on Marine Parade to serenade 101 year old Miss Margaret Russell.

In August 1980 Appledore carnival boasted the 'Pirates' dressed as 'Benson's Convicts' (Benson was a Barnstaple MP who was paid to transport convicts to North America but decided that dumping them on Lundy was more economic!)

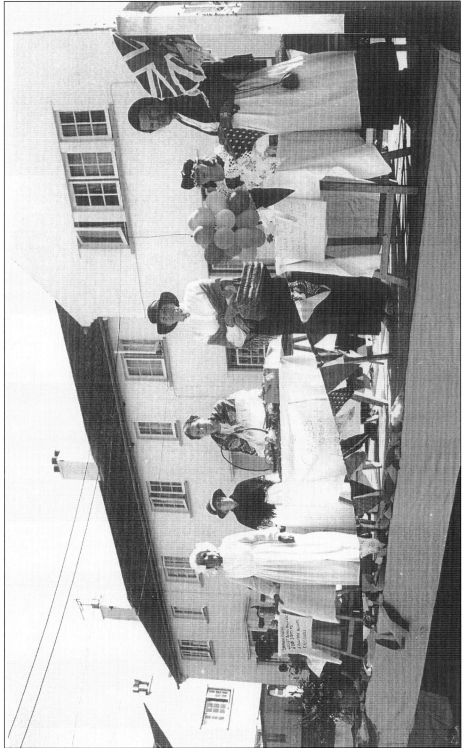

Another Appledore Carnival shot this time from August 1987. It shows the local Women's Institute float which was based on the theme of an 'Olde Market' and featured lots of old-fashioned sweets with prices to match.

Pictured here in July 1990 is the Duke of Kent mounting the Quay steps in Appledore after visiting the local lifeboat in his capacity as President of the RNLI. Landing by helicopter at Appledore Football Club's ground he was whisked off to meet Mrs.Mary Dart the first female chair of Torridge District Council and Northam's Mayor Keith Evers. After a 20 minute trip in the George Gibson lifeboat the Duke flew on to Ilfracombe but before he went a large rat suddenly appeared amongst the assembled dignitaries but was swiftly killed by Johnny Mitchell who was given the title 'Rat Catcher - By Appointment' by local people!

These two gentlemen were members of the Appledore bell-ringing team pictured
in 1905. Sitting is Jack Tawton and next to him is Mr.Down. Bell-ringing was a very
competitive sport at the time with many local teams involved but as Appledore
didn't have any church bells until 1909 these men probably rang at Northam.

Appledore Football Club sometime in the early 1950s. They are, back row, left to right; ?, Rev.Muller, Mr. Screech, Jack Griffiths, Jack Spry, Bernard Brennan, 'Bimbo' Hocking, Butler, Sammy Guard, Reg Redcliffe, Fred Harris, 'Cocky' Lamey. Front row,; Albert Beer, Bill Bates, Popham, Leo Lamey, Norman Gale, Dennis Lesslie, 'Chum' Bale, Harry Bale, ?.

This shot from April 1967 shows a goal line scramble in a match between Appledore and Ilfracombe who were competing for the Brayford Cup at Appledore's ground. In the picture the player to the left is Appledore's Clive Barber whilst the two Ilfracombe forwards (in hooped socks) are Dave Huxtable and Frank Ovey.

# Northam

*Above:* Northam Square looking deserted around 1905. The central drain in the middle of the street is obvious whilst the overhanging second storey of the building in the centre is thought to have later collapsed into the road - luckily without any injuries.

*Previous page:* . This aerial view of Northam's town centre was probably taken in the 1920s and shows the Square virtually empty of traffic. The cottages that used to stand just behind the post office were removed to widen the road and a few other small changes have occurred but the view is essentially the same one would see today.

*Previous page:* This building still stands in Northam's Fore Street - minus its outside steps which were removed in the 1930s. It is a very ancient structure its second floor having served for many years as the parish vestry room where local landowners met to run parochial affairs. The ground floor used to be a 'lock-up' (note the solid doors). It has also been a school, a cafe, a barber's shop and an off-licence before being converted to a private house.

*Above:* A later shot of the old Vestry room in a later incarnation as the Norman Café which clearly shows how buildings are constantly refurbished and re-used.

This building still stands in Northam Square but here, from around 1900, we see its original use as the village school. This was given to Northam as a school in 1852 by Mrs. Elizabeth Thorold. It had originally been a poor house but was converted into a school and teacher's house with a new front being added to the building. Today the structure is split into two with flats on the left and above the leisure centre on the right. The gates to the church along with their central pillar and the cobblestones have all disappeared.

The railings on the left help locate this view which dates from around 1900. They were surrounding the Congregational chapel in Northam Square. The small thatched cottage in the centre was at the entrance to North Street but has now been replaced by modern housing.

The houses are still there but the hedge and wall on the left have been removed to widen the road. This is Churchill Way around 1910 with its solitary gas lamp and complete absence of parked cars.

The spread of the bicycle in the late nineteenth century revolutionised transport for the masses of working people in the country. Not only did it allow easy movement to work it also gave people the opportunity to see the countryside - and many small cycle shops developed. This one was in Northam's Fore Street around 1910 - with the old vestry building shown earlier adjoining.

Cross Street, Northam is still recognizable today - just. The horse in the left foreground is patiently waiting outside the old blacksmith's forge. The large building in the centre left was Northam's second Post Office kept by Mr.Harman. The postcard is postmarked August 1908.

The Southern end of Fore Street, Northam around 1900. The junior school on the right still survives as the village Community Centre whilst the long established butcher's in the centre of the shot only finally disappeared around 1988-9 when Selwyn Raymont moved his business to the Square.

*Fore Street, Northam.*

This highly detailed view of the Southern section of Fore Street shows the newsagent's shop that replaced the cycle shop shown earlier. The man in the white coat standing in the middle was there to help children crossing the road.

The Post Office in Northam Square before it became Heath's Stores and later the post office. The bakery was run by the Burch family for some sixty years and is seen here around 1900.

*Pimpley Road, Northam.*

You may not recognise the place or the name but this is Sandymere Road under its earlier title prior to any building taking place - other than just one bungalow whose corner can be spotted on the right.

Lakenham Hill before it was widened for motor traffic. The view was taken looking down from Lakenham which later became a retirement home for elderly nuns. Within the last ten years two of the large trees on the right have been removed.

This general view of Northam probably dates from the 1920s and shows the view of the village from Lakenham Hill. Note the absence of buildings on either side of the road apart from the wall of the vicarage garden on the right.

4967. Northam from Westward Ho Road.

The same view in the 1950s after development on both sides of the road. The barn that later became St.Margaret's Court is clearly seen in the centre left of the photograph.

2146 Burrows Terrace, Bear Hill, Northcote.

This road although labelled on this 1930s postcard as Burrows Road started life as Pimpley Road and is known today as Sandymere Road. The house with its splendid greenhouse is still in existence.

This view is of the same road as the preceding one but looking down it sometime in the early 1950s. Morwenna estate and St.Margaret's school (built 1968) were later to fill the area behind the houses.

The Square, Northam

NTM.7

Northam Square again but looking towards today's Post Office. Then it was Heath's Stores and grocers. What might strike us as unexpected today are the two houses next to and set back from the Stores which were removed in the 1960s to aid the traffic flow at this very dangerous corner

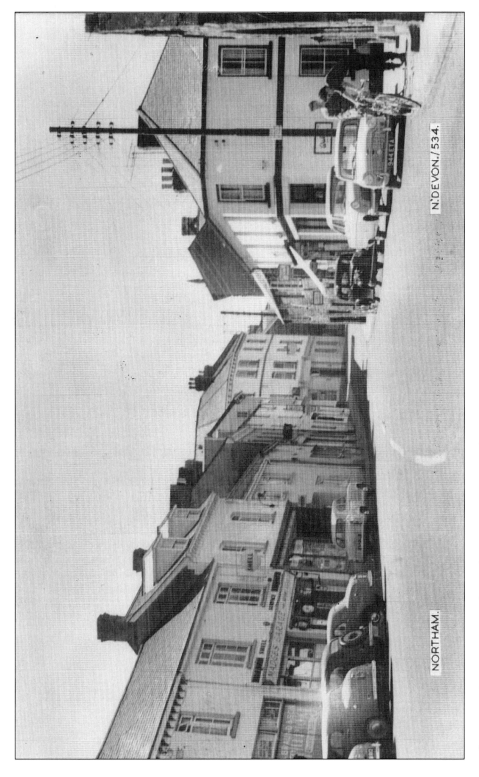

NORTHAM.

N.DEVON./534.

The general appearance of Northam Square is much the same as today in this 1960s photograph but note the existence of Madge's Garage where today's Costcutter supermarket stands. Next door is Braund's bakery - and note the absence of any yellow lines!

Northam from Windmill Lane

NTM.5

Windmill Lane in Northam with today's council offices on the right. At this date (in the early 1960s) Cross Street was the main thoroughfare to Appledore from Northam and there was no road past the present swimming pool.

North Street in Northam once acted as the back way to Appledore. The houses are still there but as is so often the case the ornamental railings seen here were taken for the 'war effort'.

Looking up Fore Street in Northam early in the 1950s. At the top is W.Watt's butcher's shop and next to it Littlejohn Brothers who advertised themselves as 'Builders and Undertakers'. The bay-windowed premises at bottom left were then a radio and electrical shop - today it is a hairdresser's. The buildings are mostly unchanged today - including the very tall chimney which indicates a previously thatched roof.

These Nissen huts were erected in Sandymere Road during the Second World War to house military personnel. After the war ended there was a huge housing shortage and so they became temporary accommodation for the homeless. The sign by the road reads 'Danger. Tanks crossing. Please drive slow'.

This bare expanse of fields is unrecognizable today as it provided the site for Richmond Park in Northam. The date is 1965 - note the two buildings on the left actually in the course of construction. The tower-like building in the foreground is part of Tadworthy Farm.

This old barn still exists today having been converted into a series of mews houses by local architect David Lott. The old Bone Hill shelter is just peeping out at the left end of the barn whilst the flagpole looms over the building.

*Above*: If you were brave enough to climb the tower of St.Margaret's church in Northam this is what you would see looking down over the Kingsley pub and the old Junior School. This particular shot dates from the mid-1970s and clearly shows evidence of the varying types of architecture that have gone to make up present day Northam.

*Below*: Look the other way and the rest of central Northam would come into view. Admiral's Court is still a long way in the future and the Richards family are running what later became the Costcutter store.

This busy scene was snapped in Northam Square around 1910. Note that the 6 wheeled open top car at the front with the luxurious looking leather seating. The roof on the right seems to consist of decomposing thatch badly in need or either removal or replacement with slates.

Before charabancs brought trippers to Westward Ho! this is how they arrived. This postcard was sent from Torrington in 1907 and records a day trip to the resort. It must have been a bumpy ride but they all look cheerful.

*Above:* This desolate looking craft was the m.v. *Lerina*, an ex-Lowestoft drifter that used to be the Lundy supply vessel. When Martin Harman purchased Lundy in 1925 for £16,000 he also got the boat and its captain Frederick Dark. During the war the vessel saw action as a P.o.W transporter and a Royal Navy auxiliary patrol vessel being one of the vessels used in secret experiments to lay an oil pipeline from Britain to France following D-Day.

*Next page:* These two fascinating photographs show differing views of Northam's first motor bus around 1912. As is clear the vehicle was built in Luton and was operated by R.Dymond from his offices in Mill Street in Bideford. Note the absence of any protection from the weather for the driver, the solid wheels, the elaborate horn and the rather precarious looking outside stairs.

In 1966 Northam town council splashed out some £2150 to buy North Devon's first mechanical road sweeper - seen here just outside Northam town hall. Today a photograph taken at the same spot would show a line of parked cars - which makes the use of such machines today virtually impossible! Ah - progress.

*Next page (top)*: These road works were being carried out in January 1967 on the route linking Bideford to Northam. If this set up looks unfamiliar to the thousands using the road today that is because the road was changed again to run to the right of the house in the centre of the picture when the new Torridge Bridge was built in 1987.

*Next page (bottom)*: When this photograph appeared in the local press it was simply titled '12 tons of washing powder overboard'. It dates from November 1968 and shows the result of a lorry crash in Northam at the junction of Leigh Crescent and Cross Street. Owned by W.J.Lamey & Sons of Appledore there were no injuries - other than to the packets of Fairy Snow washing powder.

Bone Hill possibly showing the Northam 'Revels' sometime around 1910. The swing boats may look primitive to us but they were a very exciting 'ride' for Edwardian youngsters.

*Above and next page:* These three photographs show stages in the construction of the Torridge Bridge. The first dates from January 1985 and shows the first temporary structures going out into the river from the Northam side. The next dates from September of that year and shows that considerable progress had been made. Note the presence of the now demolished Bideford Shipyard on the left. The third picture is from a month later and illustrates how the basic low level construction work was progressing.

*Above*: A very pristine looking Bone Hill with its shelter. The scheme to tidy up this area which used to house a 'holy well' and a rubbish dump was carried out in 1867 and funded by Thomas Pynsent and J.Gordon and many local people partly to clear up this area and partly to provide work for the unemployed - at a cost of £51.37

*Below*: The Boy Scouts movement was started by Lord Baden-Powell in 1906. The 16th North Devon Troop based in Northam began life in 1912. These Scouts actually guarded the airbase on Northam Burrows in the First World War.

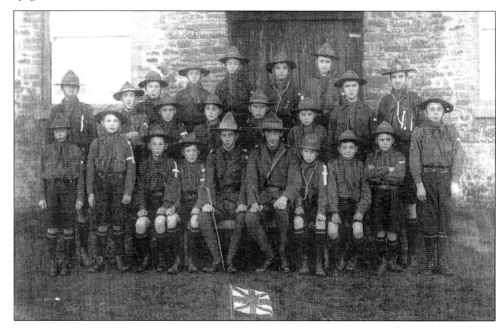

These keen looking but rather elderly gentlemen were some of the early volunteers in the First World War version of the Home Guard - the Civil Volunteer Corps. They were pictured in front of the chapel in Northam Square and several are wearing armbands with a 'C' visible including C.F. Saunders the man in the bowler hat in the second row.

This crowded scene shows the dedication of the Northam war memorial in 1920. The vicar was the Reverend Payne Cook. The very rare statue which is very similar to New York's Statue of Liberty has yet to be put in place on top of the plinth. The monument listed the names of those who gave their lives in World War One.

The coronation of Queen Elizabeth II in 1953 saw celebratory street parties in every community - including this one at Morwenna Park in Northam which has long had a strong community spirit. Every child is wearing a party hat and notice the four babies in their high chairs at the front.

Northam Church choir in the 1950s standing in front of the highly ornamented western door of St.Margaret's. The choristers are, from left to right; B.Hancock, J.H.Uglow, Syd Hookway, Charlie Mounce, Billy Gale, E.Kelly, Christopher and Alan Jewell.

This photograph dates from July 1969 and shows another 'good idea' that never came to fruition. Paul Sherlock is seen here demonstrating a dry-ski run before members of Northam town council and the local Chamber of Commerce in the hope that the two bodies would fund it as a new tourist attraction. Whatever happened to this we wonder?

*Above*: This shot shows St.Margaret's school in Northam celebrating the Queen's Silver Jubilee in 1977. The flagpole in the picture also doubled up as the school's maypole.

*Next page*: The Torridge Swimming Pool in Northam is a well used facility and this photograph from May 1987 shows part of the opening celebrations. Torridge district council had invited Duncan Goodhew, Britain's foremost swimmer, to do the honours and here he is seen diving into the pool in front of a very appreciative audience.

The Bishop of Crediton heads a procession of children from St.Margaret's school at Northam in April 1984 to open the newly refurbished 'Upper Room' in the corner of the churchyard. This 'Room' was the old mortuary which played host to the many drowned seamen who were washed up on the Westward Ho! pebble ridge.

# Westward Ho!

**"WESTWARD HO" HOTEL - THE SEA FRONT.**

FOUNDATION STONE LAID BY THE COUNTESS OF PORTSMOUTH, FEB 8TH 1864.

*Above*: The Westward Ho! Hotel, as it was first called was begun in February 1864 when the Countess of Portsmouth laid the foundation stone and opened in June 1865. It later changed its name to the Royal Hotel and even later to the Golden Bay - whilst today it has been replaced by apartments under the name Ocean Park.

*Next page*: To go with the earlier aerial views of Appledore and Northam is this one of Westward Ho! with Kipling and Kingsley Terraces dominating the centre of the picture. The very open nature of early Westward Ho! is clearly seen in this shot from the late 1920s/early 1930s.

WESTWARD HO FROM AN AEROPLANE. (4639)

Another photograph of the Westward Ho! (Golden Bay) Hotel - this time showing a fine view of the tennis court around the 1920s - an area that has now been built over.

GOLDEN BAY HOTEL, WESTWARD HO.

The Golden Bay Hotel here stands proudly isolated on a postcard from 1929. The hotel catered to an up-market clientele and was demolished only a few years ago - yet another loss of accommodation in the resort.

Another shot shows the seaward side of the Hotel with the later extension to the left. The large scale of the enterprise comes over well on this postcard which was postally used in 1926.

The Pebble Ridge Hotel was built to cater for the growing number of tourists to the resort and as was common in those days the hotel bore the name of the man who ran it - in this case Mr.Kemp.

The Westward Ho! cricket pavilion on the left helps locate this picture which is included to show where the Pebble Ridge Hotel stood. The second shot shows the destruction of the once-proud building in September 1993. The bungalows to the right still exist.

Stand on the Westward Ho! Pebble Ridge and look back today and this view would be very different as Nelson Terrace which dominates this photograph has disappeared behind later commercial structures. This postcard was postally used in September 1904.

Nelson Terrace in Westward Ho! was started as a row of shops in 1865 but owing to a financial 'hiccup' wasn't completed for some years. The wrought iron balconies have now disappeared apparently having been taken to help the 'war effort'. At the time this photograph was taken around 1910 the buildings had an uninterrupted view of the sea but this has long gone as development mushroomed in the resort.

HIGH STREET, WESTWARD HO.

We are unsure when Nelson Terrace was ever known as High Street but clearly the manufacturers of this postcard believed this was its name. Note the absence of any cars - so different to today's street scene.

*Above:* Looking the other way from Nelson Terrace. The shops are still recognisable even if the houses in the middle have all gone. The photograph is hard to date but the first cars that were to later dominate the scene are here.

*Next page:* Eastbourne Terrace in Westward Ho! was built as high class accommodation for the first wave of residents in the expanding resort. The grand houses are still instantly recognisable today even though they have become marooned amidst modern development.

Eastbourne Terrace, Westward Ho! 8

Dyer, Torrington.

*Above:* Eastbourne Terrace today is full of parked cars unlike in this shot from the late 1920s which shows cows from a local dairy grazing along the roadside.

*Next page:* Few would recognise this view today even though many people drive and walk along it daily. It shows Atlantic Way in Westward Ho! around 1920 bordered by the still existing but lowered wall enclosing the gardens at Lakenham.

View from Northam Rd. Westward Ho.

59349

The Furshills, Northam.

The 'emptiness' of early Westward Ho! is well shown in this very striking photograph which has Beach Road running down to Eastbourne Terrace and Venton Farm through empty fields with none of the massive developments which came later.

This rather Spartan looking building was the Westward Ho! Junior School around 1900 when R.J.Leakey MA was the Headmaster. It had been established by the United Services College in a private house at Buckleigh in 1879 but moved into these premises in 1880. The picture actually shows the rear view of the establishment which stood above the USC (now Kipling Terrace). It became a country club in 1947 and was partly demolished and partly re-built in 1975.

Looking down across Westward Ho! sometime in the 1920s we see the small 'Octagon' building which had once stood on Bideford Quay and beyond it the as yet underdeveloped area that later housed the Fairway Buoy public house and two amusement arcades. The need for a sea wall to prevent erosion is well shown in the shot. The new Nautilus development now stands where the 'Octagon' once stood.

*High Tide, Westward Ho.*

This striking photograph shows the openness of Westward Ho! to erosion by the sea. It was precisely because of storms and high tides like the one shown here that the coastal defence wall was begun in 1928. The houses in this shot were part of Westbourne Terrace.

The Dormy House was another tourist development which provided accommodation for golfers attracted to the Links at Westward Ho! It was built in 1938 and later changed its name to the Atlanta and was burnt down in 1970.

GOLF LINKS ROAD, WESTWARD HO.

21842 4.J.V.

The appearance of the development on the left of this view has changed out of all recognition. Dating probably from the 1930s it shows some of the early holiday growth in the resort.

THE FRONT, WESTWARD HO!

2302

The row of houses on the front at Westward Ho! in the 1950s before they were all converted into shops. Note the price of car parking in the Northam Urban District Council facility - just 6d or 2.5p!

Westward Ho! constantly re-invents itself - at the expense of its existing buildings. This shot shows the remains of Teddy Bazell's leather goods shop following its demolition in August 1989. The site now houses the waiting area for local bus services.

*Above:* This photograph from December 1979 shows the knocking down of the Kingsley Leisure Centre that stood in Golf Links Road after its very short life as a tourist attraction. The site has now been developed as permanent housing.

*Next page:* One of the latest ideas in Westward Ho! is the redevelopment of the large grounds surrounding the old grand houses - as with Broomhayes in this photograph which also shows the huge amount of earth movements involved.

*Above:* This, although not technically brilliant, is one of the earliest pictures we have of Westward Ho! and its famous Pebble Ridge. The two ladies in their crinolines and with sunshades accompany a top hatted man for a walk along the beach. The shot was taken where the Ridge curves round still today - but the absence of any buildings makes it difficult to orientate ourselves. The ghost-like building behind them is probably the old Lower Lodge which had to be moved inland as the Ridge retreated.

*Next page:* The pier at Westward Ho! was begun by the grandly named Northam Burrows and Landing Pier Company in 1864. It took two attempts to complete finally opening in July 1873 but was soon destroyed by the sea - finally going in 1880 leaving just some iron stumps of the piers behind.

WESTWARD HO PIER
ABOUT 1870.

High tide at the Pebble Ridge sometime before the First World War. Notice the large tents used for changing into swimming costumes long before the sea wall and arcade developments arrived.

Westward Ho.    9081

Clearly this is the 'front' at Westward Ho! but notice the absence of promenade wall, the putting green and any shelter. The small 'Octagon' building is just visible having been transplanted from Bideford. The postcard this illustration comes from was posted in 1935.

This slightly faded photograph dates from around the same date and shows a very ornate hut just on the left. The coastal defence wall is yet to be built and the whole scene appears to be a very English hotch-potch of small, eccentric buildings.

A close-up of one of the huts from the 1920s. This was a splendid example - with stained glass (!) and a stout looking roof. This isn't surprising given that it belonged to the Cock family of Bideford who were notable builders. From left to right the people were Florence Cock, Christine Cock, Netty Penwarden, Douglas Cock, Herbert Penwarden and Vernon Cock.

A photograph probably dating from the early 1920s shows Westward Ho! front with the Bath Hotel in the centre of the picture and Kipling Tors behind. The erosion of the cliff in front of what is today's green open space and the destruction of the groynes is very obvious - and shows why a sea wall was desperately needed. The coastal defences were eventually constructed in three stages over the years 1928-31 by the long defunct Northam Urban District Council.

CHAR-A-BANCS ARRIVING AT WESTWARD HO.

What a busy scene this old postcard reveals. The 'char-a-bancs' were the buses of the first decades of the twentieth century and doubtless the shops already present in this photograph were glad to see them arrive. On the gable of the tea shop on the extreme left is a sign reading 'Motor Park' - a rather attractive name for the humble car park.

The Braddick family has long connections with Westward Ho! and today run the main holiday facilities in the resort. Even they had to begin somewhere, however, and this wonderful shot shows their first 'holiday camp' made up of tents and decommissioned buses in 1933. Kipling Tors rises up behind and though it looks primitive to us we have no doubt that early tourists enjoyed their seaside breaks as much as we do today

Form AR—E.

## REGISTRATION FORM
(For use in Hotels, Inns, Lodging-houses, etc., under the provisions of Article 7 of the Aliens Order.)

**British subjects need fill in only 1, 2, 3, and 4 of Part I, and sign it. Aliens must complete the whole form and sign both Parts.**

Postal address of Hotel, Inn or Lodging-house, etc... *Golfstead, Eastbourne Terrace, Westward Ho, N. Devon,*

### PART I
TO BE FILLED IN IMMEDIATELY ON ARRIVAL

1. Surname ___SHIELD___    2. Christian Names ___Louisa___

3. Nationality ___British___    4. Date of arrival ___26. 8. 1940___.

5. Sex (M. or F.) ___F___

6. Particulars of Registration Certificate or Passport:

  * Registration Certificate/Passport issued at_____ ; No._____

7. Arrived here from (give last address in full)___6 Southmead Rd.___
___Filton, Bristol.___

Signature of person to whom } ___Louisa Shield___
the above particulars relate }

* *Please strike out as necessary.*    [For Part II see overleaf.

---

*Above and below:* Even during the war tourism, albeit on a much reduced scale, continued though visitors had to fill in various forms as shown here for a b&b in Eastbourne Terrace.

---

*Continuation of Form AR—E]*

### PART II
TO BE FILLED IN ON DEPARTURE

8. Date of departure...........................

9. New address or destination .....................
  (give new address in full)

Signature of person to whom }
the above particulars relate }

**PENALTY FOR FAILING TO FURNISH THE REQUIRED INFORMATION OR FOR GIVING FALSE INFORMATION—£100 FINE OR 6 MONTHS' IMPRISONMENT.**

LONDON
PUBLISHED BY HIS MAJESTY'S STATIONERY OFFICE

To be purchased directly from H.M. STATIONERY OFFICE at the following addresses : York House, Kingsway, London, W.C.2 ; 120 George Street, Edinburgh 2 ; 26 York Street, Manchester 1 ; 1 St. Andrew's Crescent, Cardiff ; 80 Chichester Street, Belfast ; or through any bookseller.

Price 1d. net, or 50 for 6d. net, or 1000 for 6s. 0d. net.

Printed under the authority of His Majesty's Stationery Office by Metcalfe & Cooper, Ltd., London.

100m 3/40 [78309] 1562/— 100m 6/40 M&C Ltd. 706    S.O. Code No. 34-9999

THE STAGE AT THE WESTWARD HO HOLIDAY CENTRE. N. DEVON.

The Westward Ho! Holiday Centre was better known as Top Camp having been built in just 3 months by a work force up to 600 strong at times. Opened on 30 June 1939 by 'Britain's No.1 out-door star' Belle Chrystall the camp was soon commandeered by the government to house Army personnel and displaced persons during the war. After 1945 it re-opened and became very popular - until its still lamented closure

Top Camp boasted a large number of attractions as shown on this rare postcard produced to celebrate Queen Elizabeth II's coronation in 1953 .

TORVILLE CARAVAN CAMP

As Westward Ho! developed so caravan parks mushroomed in the 1950s including the Torville Camp at Golf Links Road. The site is now completely built over by the Fairways and Ridgeways developments.

THE SANDS, WESTWARD HO!

H 8930

Taking a ride on the ponies used to be a highlight for many visitors to Westward Ho! as this postcard from the late 1950s shows. The gentleman to the right who ran the business was Mr. Holman - whilst his daughter 'Bubbles' is on the pony on the left.

The BBC's Radio 1 channel used to regularly tour Britain's coastal resorts staging a 'Roadshow'. Westward Ho! was visited and here from August 1987 we see DJ Bruno Brookes with a few lucky youngsters in the control booth - with a 2000 strong crowd of holidaymakers and locals in the background. The girl with the headphones on was Beth Neal of Northam.

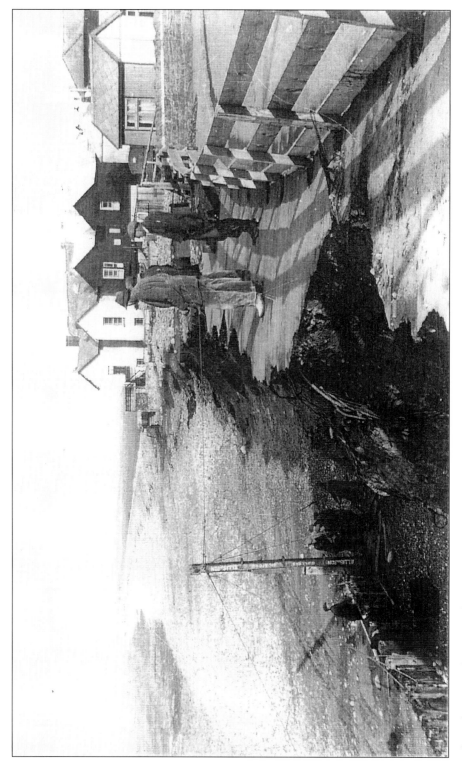

This photograph comes from a glass negative and shows work going on in the late 1920s at Westward Ho! to construct a line of wooden piles in front of a badly eroded cliff edge. The end of Westbourne Terrace is behind the three men on the right.

A few years later in 1930 with the piles in place construction of the sea wall began. The central part is already in place but the rest is being built - there are some nine men shown. Note the miniature tramway built along the beach to help them move heavy material. Also note the breakwater, one of six, on the left designed to blunt the force of the waves.

The Bath Hotel in Westward Ho! appears in this shot from 1929. It was built in 1867 and contained a Ladies' Swimming Bath 'supplied from the sea by Steam Engines' which, it was claimed, was 'an excellent place for young ladies to learn to swim.' The photograph also catches some of the famously varied beach huts on a coastal 'wall' made up of stacked pebbles.

*Above:* Potwalloping was an old custom whereby Northam residents went down to the Pebble Ridge at Westward Ho! and using carts and muscle power replaced all the stones that had been thrown onto the Burrows by the sea. The earliest reference we have come across appears in the *North Devon Journal* for December 1845. The event in October 1851 was described as being 'carried on in good earnest, and by the exertions of a large number of people.' This photograph shows a group around 1920.


*Next page:* A crowded scene from around 1920 showing a no-doubt welcome break in the potwalloping activity. Local farmers provided the horses and carts seen in the photograph - along with the refreshments.

The constant problem for Westward Ho! over many years has been the attack of the sea on the Pebble Ridge and the repeated inundation of the Burrows behind. These dramatic photographs show one such breach - and its aftermath. We are uncertain of the date but would suggest 1947.

A later breach is shown in the photograph which dates from 1962. The local council has mobilised earth moving vehicles to move pebbles into the 'gap'. Such emergency measures have, so far, preserved the Ridge and the land behind but with global warming and a consequent rise in sea level one has to wonder for how much longer?

*Above:* The power of the storms is such that the promenade at Westward Ho! often looks like this - with heavy pebbles littered all over it. This photograph, which dates from the 1970s, shows the old play equipment that used to be found on the 'Triangle' next to the amusement arcade seen in the background.

*Next page:* Potwalloping changed over the years and here we see what it looked like in 2000 when celebrations had moved from the Pebble Ridge to the Putting Green. Sadly the whole *raison d'etre* has been destroyed by the dreaded 'health and safety' rules which now forbid the throwing back of stones on to the Ridge. Such is life.

Train en Route, Westward Ho. Published by Wills, Mill Street, Bideford ~ Photo, Sanders, Bideford

The Bideford-Westward Ho! Railway was opened in May 1901 (the Appledore section didn't get built until 1908) and here we see it in the Kenwith Valley at Northam just after leaving Bideford on a postcard produced by a local firm.

These two very rare pieces of railway ephemera come from the short lived but much loved Bideford, Westward Ho! and Appledore railway. The timetable, although dated 1905, includes the Appledore section even though it had yet to be built.

This charming picture of the Bideford, Westward Ho! and Appledore Railway shows a group of boater-wearing men 'taking the air' at the rear of a First Class carriage around 1910. The railway, of course, only lasted a very brief time (1901-17) and its final resting place is still unknown today.

## WESTWARD HO!

This rather murky but fascinating shot shows the old Bideford & Westward Ho! railway line. Kipling Tors looks strangely bare whilst Seafield and today's 'Pier House' are clearly seen in the centre of the picture.

Some seventy years after it disappeared a memorial plaque to the Bideford, Westward Ho! and Appledore railway was unveiled on the wall which is the final remnant of the Appledore station in Torridge Road. This particular station was opened on April 23 1908 and only operated for nine years. The lady doing the unveiling is Mrs.Mabel Payne. The plaque has been replaced in turn by a large terracotta panel designed and made by Maggi Curtis.

Visitors to Westward Ho! and locals alike will remember this rather incongruous looking little building. It was a railway signal box in a back garden. According to research by Clive Fairchild it probably originated from Maddaford Moor Halt near Okehampton. After the First World War a traction engine is supposed to have transported the building to this resting place. Here it stayed for many years but was sold a few years ago to a railway enthusiast at Newbury.

The dangers of the North Devon coastline to mariners are well shown in this very striking photograph of the wreck of the *Madeline* a French schooner which went ashore at Westward Ho! in 1908. Luckily no lives were lost.

This wonderful photograph shows a decommissioned Royal Navy torpedo boat HMS *Sandfly* (note the torpedo tubes amidships) ashore on the Pebble Ridge at Westward Ho! on 11 January 1921. She was being towed to South Wales when she broke loose and ended up ashore.

Jeremy Thorpe, one-time MP for North Devon, was always noted for his flamboyance - indeed some would say it helped lead to his spectacular downfall following a national scandal he was involved in. Back in 1974, however, the colourful MP set off on a hovercraft tour of coastal areas of North Devon. This photograph shows him arriving at Westward Ho! where about 2000 holidaymakers gathered to see this very unusual craft.

This wonderful photograph shows one of the first cars in North Devon. It was taken in 1903 and shows Charles Stent flanked to the right by his mother Mrs. Sterling Stent and to the left by Maggie Slade. Charles set up the first garage at Westward Ho! and was Westcountry agent for White's Steam Cars - one of which he is driving here.

Telegrams : " Stent," Westward Ho !

Phone **29.**                    Agent for

Commercial Union Assurance Co.
Motor Union Insurance Co.
British Dominions Insurance Co.
Warden Insurance Co.

# STENT'S GARAGE,

(C. E. STENT, M.I.A.E., Proprietor),

## WESTWARD HO! N. DEVON.

Cars Bought and Sold.        **REPAIRS**        Tyres, Oils, Petrol, etc.

Private Lock-ups.        Cars for Hire.        Supplied.

Michelin and Dunlop Tyre Stockists.

This business card gives some idea of Mr. Stent's business acumen - and note the telephone number - a simple '29'.

Mr. Stent's garage is shown here around the mid-1920s - a building that only disappeared in the last couple of years when the site was given over to new housing.

This astonishing photograph has an inscription on the reverse which reads '1920. The last coach to run in Bideford. Photograph taken in Golf Links Road Westward Ho! Driver J.Parsons. Guard J.H.Parsons, Orchard Hill, Bideford.'

No5 'GENERAL VIEW N.D.H. I.Y. CAMP WESTWARD HO! 1908

A close-up view of the North Devon Hussars/Imperial Yeomanry camp at Westward Ho! in 1908 when they carried out annual training under the watchful eye of General Sir Ian Hamilton. The photograph was produced by W.Wood of Bear Street in Barnstaple.

The local Territorial forces often exercised in the area. This first photograph shows a field kitchen possibly at Cornborough with a temporary bread oven in front - and note the sign for 'A.Reed, Baker, Appledore' who was based in Bude Street in the village and was clearly good at spotting a marketing opportunity.

Devon Yeo.Bde. R.F.A. Westward-Ho. 1922.

37.

This second shot shows a camp held at Westward Ho! by the Devon Yeomanry Brigade of the Royal Field Artillery in 1922. The horse-drawn artillery is evidence that the Army had yet to become motorised.

Here's something the average beachcomber doesn't expect to find! It was the body of an unfortunate whale washed ashore at Westward Ho! (Bath Hotel is in the background) in the 1920s. Apparently the smell from the rotting corpse did nothing to help the local tourist industry.

Copyright
W. Ho. 91.

Golf Course, Westward Ho.

Raphael Tuck & Sons Ltd
London.

The Royal North Devon Golf Club can trace its history back to 1864 and its club house is shown in this 1930s photograph. It holds a magnificent collection of golfing history.

J.H.Taylor was a Northam resident who began caddying at Westward Ho! in the 1870s and went on to become Open Champion on five occasions as well as winning the French Championship twice and the German once. This card has his address 23 Windmill Lane, Northam on the back as well as his telephone number 'Northam 77'.

The plus-fours and ancient looking golf club in this photograph are deceptive. It was taken in May 1964 and shows professional Max Faulkner taking part in an 'old and new' match at Westward Ho! Max and fellow pro Christie O'Connor were using hickory shafted clubs dating back to 1864 in a match against Peter Alliss and Brian Huggett who were using modern clubs. Needless to say the round scores reflected the advance in technology - Alliss 73, Huggett 76, O'Connor 83 and Faulkner 90.

This splendid selection of youngsters in fancy dress were attending a party at the Westward Ho! Top Camp in 1953 held to mark the Coronation of Queen Elizabeth II. The ingenuity on display in creating the variety of costumes is inspiring even if some of them might not be seen as politically correct today.

Westward Ho! Womens' Institute entered this float 'For Home and Country' in the resort's carnival in 1957. The ladies were, from left to right, Mrs.Pope, Mrs.Moore, Mrs.Bishop, Miss Wood, Mrs.Day, Mrs.Poultney and Miss Masters.

In August 1964 locals at Westward Ho! organised a series of pony races on the beach - with the Pebble Ridge doing duty as a handy 'grandstand'. This photograph shows the Braddick Cup Race where B.Heard on 'Settler' just pipped J.Rogers on 'Toy Fair' to win. Other events included the Atlantic Sands Trailer Park Race, the Torville Camp Race and the James Boys Bakery Race.

In the last days of February 1967 massive gales whipped up mountainous seas all around the coast of North Devon leading to the disappearance of three gardens at Appledore. Much of the sand on Westward Ho! beach was stripped off - revealing four Second World War mines which had to be blown up by a bomb disposal squad. The photograph shows David Garden (on right) who discovered them, Sergeant Reg Reeves, P.C. David Greenaway and *Journal-Herald* reporter Leslie Petherbridge.

Famously Westward Ho! was the home of the United Services College. Opened in September 1874 in a row of 12 terraced villas which still exist today it continued in the village until 1904 when it was moved nearer London. Its most famous pupil was Rudyard Kipling (there 1878-82) though Bruce Bairnsfeather the famous World War I comic artist was also an 'old boy'. This photograph shows some of the pupils in a cricket team from around 1890. Names are as follows; back row, left to right, H.S.Browne, C.C.Mullon, G.H.Hives II, F.W.Garnett. Front row, J.Budgen, H.W.Disney-Rocknote (?), E.K.Little, J.Hensbrow (?), N.B.Fellowes, R.C.Seddon and, sitting in front, E.Pocklington.

*Lazarus Press*
Bideford